Cartoons for Trainers

Cartoons for Trainers

Seventy-Five Cartoons to Use or Adapt
for Transitions, Activities, Discussion Points,
Ice-Breakers and More

Lenn Millbower

Cartoons by Doris Yager

Sterling, Virginia

Published in 2002 by

Stylus Publishing, LLC
22883 Quicksilver Drive
Sterling, Virginia 20166

Library of Congress Cataloging-in-Publication Data

Millbower, Lenn, 1951–
Cartoons for traniers : seventy-five cartoons to use or adapt for
transitions, activities, discussion points, ice-breakers and more / Lenn
Millbower ; cartoons by Doris Yager.
    p. cm
  ISBN 1-57922-055-X (pbk. with CD-ROM : alk. paper)
1. Comic books, strips, etc. in education. 2. Training—Caricatures
and cartoons. I. Yager, Doris, ill. II. Title.
  LB1044.9.C59 .M55 2002
    371.33—dc21   2001008454

First edition, 2002

Printed in the United States of America

All first editions printed on acid free paper

This book is dedicated to two individuals who have had profound influences on our lives; Rebecca Millbower and Robert Scheideman.

To my lovely wife Rebecca: Your infectious laugh inspires me daily.

Lenn Millbower

To my father Robert Scheideman: You would be so happy to know that I have finally fulfilled your dream by swaying from the dance world and putting into motion my artistic skills.

Doris Yager

Licensing Agreement

Please read this document as carefully as you would any legal document. If you determine that you cannot abide by the conditions of this licensing agreement, you may return Cartoons for Trainers with proof of purchase to Stylus Publishing within seven (7) days for a full refund.

1. Copyright Cartoons for Trainers, including both the book and the attached CD-ROM contains cartoons that are provided under license. Cartoons for Trainers is copyrighted by Stylus Publishing, LLC.

2. License Stylus Publishing, LLC grants to the purchaser a non-exclusive license to use the cartoons in accordance with the terms of this license.

3. Photocopying Cartoons The cartoons printed in the book may only be copied onto overhead projection film. The cartoon CD-ROM images may only be used on one computer or projection system at a time. Site licenses can be obtained for an additional fee by contacting Stylus Publishing, LLC.

4. Distributing Cartoons Under no circumstances, is distribution of the cartoons allowed.

5. Altering Cartoons With the exception of adding text to the non-caption versions on the CD-ROM, alteration of the cartoons is not permitted.

6. Transfer of Ownership If ownership of a copy of Cartoons for Trainers should be transferred from one person to another, the person who gains ownership is also bound by this agreement.

7. Termination of Rights If any portions of this licensing agreement are not adhered to, Stylus Publishing, LLC reserves the right to terminate this licensing agreement and seek legal remedy, including but not limited to financial damages and punitive fines.

CD Usage Instructions

Both the Captioned and Captionless folder cartoons are provided in the JPEG format, and are placed in folders that match the book index headings. To use the cartoons in an electronic presentation, simply complete the following steps:

1. Select the cartoon you want to use from the companion book.

2. Identify that cartoon's electronic name.

3. Identify the folder where the electronic cartoon is located. (The CD folders match the book index. Use the book index as a guide to identify the appropriate folder.)

4. Insert and open the CD by following your computer's normal procedures.

5. Open the appropriate cartoon folder.

6. Insert the cartoon into your presentation by following the graphic insertion procedures as prescribed in your presentation application.

7. Add captions and other desired text (captionless cartoons only) by following the text insertion procedures described in your presentation application.

8. Save your document.

Acknowledgments

This book would not have been possible without the support and guidance of a great many people. We would like to officially acknowledge the following individuals.

Lenn Millbower   The number of people I would like to thank for affecting my life is far too numerous to list. To those people, I apologize for not mentioning your names. In contrast, some people were directly involved in the creation of this book. I wish to publicly thank those people: Doris Yager, my mentor, who brought my ideas to life; Frank Barnes, David Freeman, and John Murray at the Disney University, for encouraging the creation of this book; Dave Adelman and David Mulvey at the Disney Institute (I told you these cartoons were funny); Nan Summers, a true beacon of knowledge; John von Knorring, whose faith in the product resulted in this book being published; Larry and Denise Lessard, for the many laughs we have shared; my wife Rebecca to whom this book is dedicated; and finally, my mother who maintained her sense of humor every time I showed up on her doorstep.

Doris Yager   I would like to extend my thanks to the individuals who gave me support and encouragement throughout this project: Lenn Millbower, for the opportunity to return to the art field; Genevieve Millbower, for her long term friendship, for bringing Lenn to my entertainment company as a youngster, and for giving me the opportunity to watch his talents develop as he obtained great heights; my children and their spouses, for their enthusiasm and encouragement during this project; to Stacey, my daughter-in-law, for her communication link to Lenn in Florida and her suggestions to enhance the drawings; the Yager "research team," especially Diane, Brian, and Chelsea, for providing critical reference material; and finally, my good Rhythm-Lite friends, Genevieve, Doris and Tony DeSalvo, Charlie Taylor, and the many others from the company who rallied behind me through the years and contributed to the success of my entertainment productions. Thank you all!

Contents

Part One: Classroom Life

Introductions

Expectations

Activities

Breaks

Food

Discussions

Tests and Evaluations

Classroom Awards

Conclusions

Part Two: Training Topics

Brainstorming / Creativity

Career Development

Change

Communication Skills

Computer Based Training

Introduction

This book grew out of a need. From universities to corporate classrooms, instructors use cartoons to make learning points.

Humor is an important component in any learning environment. Even when instructors ignore humor, the learners find it, sometimes at the instructor's expense. The need for laughter is so strong that learners seek out opportunities to laugh throughout every class. The instructor who uses humor as an instructional tool will soon discover that learners respond.

But what is an instructor to do, become a comedian? Comedy is a complicated art, best practiced carefully. A far easier approach is to rely on cartoons as a vehicle for creating humor.

Cartoons permeate our lives. We encounter them in our daily newspaper comics and editorial pages, while surfing the world wide web, in magazines, animated in movies and on television, on wall and desk calendars, and through sharing at the office. It is natural and appropriate to use them in learning situations. It is, for a number of reasons, also demonstrative of solid instructional design. Those reasons include the following:

• Cartoons release tension.
• Cartoons transcend negative emotion.
• Cartoons illuminate content.
• Cartoons engage both hemispheres.
• Cartoons aid memorization.
• Cartoons build rapport.

Cartoons release tension One reason people laugh, especially in the learning environment, is to release whatever tension they feel. Humor allows people to discuss difficult subjects. Most comedy is built around the tragedies and absurdities of everyday life. Once a challenging subject is presented in a comedic fashion, the tension releases and people begin to focus on dealing with the real issues involved, instead of the emotions they are feeling.

Cartoons transcend negative emotion Studies demonstrate that strong emotions overpower the thinking regions of the brain. Most instructors have experienced situations where learners refused to learn because of negative emotions. Cartoons have the unique ability to present negative emotions in a humorous, enjoyable, and non-threatening manner that allows people to transcend the negative aspects of the situation.

Cartoons illuminate content   Laughter illuminates a subject in a way not possible through lecture alone. Humor takes a naturally occurring situation and points out the absurdities to be found in that situation. The joke takes what we expect, and turns that expectation on its head, surprising us with an equally valid, often absurd, alternative solution to the situation at hand. Cartoons add extra dimension to learning environments, illuminate the subject matter in new, unexpected ways, that challenge learners to focus on details.

Cartoons engage both hemispheres   The left hemisphere of the human brain processes information logically; the right hemisphere processes information holistically. It is apparent that cartoons offer a holistic view of a subject. What is also true, but less apparent, is that cartoons force logical processing. Jokes create humor by presenting details that seemingly lead to one logical conclusion. The humor occurs when the learner discovers that the details presented have a completely different, also logical, interpretation. This realization causes the learner to engage the logic processing abilities of the left hemisphere.

Cartoons aid memorization   A joke requires the twisting of details into new conclusions. This means that learners must, in order to get the joke, pay attention to the details. The result is that learners absorb more information when humor is present. In addition, when people see a joke they reconstruct it in their minds, causing them to repeat the material.

Cartoons build rapport   Cartoons build rapport between instructors and learners. When people laugh at the absurdities of life together, they become partners in humanity. Suddenly, they have something in common; they have discovered a way to understand, and to relate to, each other more fully.

Even with the advantages cartoons offer, utilizing them in learning environments leads to specific difficulties. Virtually all the cartoons instructors come into contact with are copyright protected. The use of these cartoons, without permission, constitutes a considerable risk. Penalties for unauthorized use violations can be costly. Permission to use individual cartoons can be obtained, but the time involved in obtaining permission does not allow for the quick use when appropriate situations occur. Even then, purchase of individual cartoons is often costly.

As instructors who value the effectiveness of cartoons we decided to do something about these challenges. We decided to create our own cartoons and package them in three different versions:

1. **Book pages sized for reproduction onto overhead film**   These cartoons can be found on the book pages. The book has been intentionally sized for reproduction.

2. **Duplicate electronic captioned cartoons for use in presentations**   Some facilitators may prefer electronic presentations to the older overhead

projector technology. With that in mind, we also placed the same cartoons, in the same order and under the same headings, on an attached CD-ROM. These versions will easily import into most of the popular presentation software products.

3. **Duplicate electronic captionless cartoons for tailoring to specific classroom situations**   Finally, we realized that the cartoon captions, the additional language in the cartoons, and even the cartoon titles that work best in our learning environment might not fit yours. To provide you with maximum flexibility, we included a duplicate set of cartoons without words. Use these cartoons to write the captions and other language that best suits your learning needs.

We divided our cartoons into two broad categories:

- Classroom Life
- Training Topics

Classroom Life

Classroom Life cartoons address the daily situations that occur in classrooms all over the world, including humorous takes on introductions, expectations, activities, breaks, food, discussions, tests and evaluations, conclusions, and classroom awards. The cartoons are designed to illuminate critical points, aid in transitions, and help learners relax and enjoy the learning environment.

Training Topics

Training Subject cartoons focus on various subjects that engage learners daily. The topics include brainstorming/creativity, career development, change, conflict, communication skills, computer-based training, customer service, diversity, HazCom, heavy machinery training, fiscal awareness, management theory, motivation, on-the-job training, orientation, safety awareness, sexual harassment, speech/presentations, stress management, teamwork, telecommunications, and time management. These cartoons, one or two per subject, are helpful in framing discussions, illustrating key subject concepts, and easing learner fears.

In the book text, we have described one usage for each cartoon. Our intent was not to dictate a specific usage, but rather to inspire you to use these cartoons in ways that suit your needs. To that end, we have provided space after each cartoon description so that you might record your own usage ideas.

Finally, we decided to offer these cartoons, properly licensed, to the training community for a reasonable price. The result is this book. Please purchase it, enjoy it, and use it (legally of course). Your learners will enjoy your classroom; they will admire you for your wit; and, most importantly, they will retain your message.

Lenn Millbower
Doris Yager

Part One

By Millbower and Yager

"The real purpose of humor in teaching is to link the pupils and the teacher, and to link them through enjoyment. When people laugh together, they cease to be young and old, master and pupil, they become a single group of human beings enjoying its existence." —Gilbert Highet. (1950). *The Art of Teaching*. New York, NY: Random House, Inc.

Classroom Life—Introductions

The Cartoon: Family History

The Captioned Folder Name: Fam_His1

The Captionless Folder Name: Fam_His2

The Subject: Overly Long Introductions.

The Action: A learner gets carried away introducing himself and shares his life story as the instructor worries about maintaining the class timeline.

The Take: Introductions should be kept short.

The Use: To set expectations regarding the length of time an introduction should take.

The Patter: "Of course we all want to learn as much as possible about each other, but we also want to learn as much class content as possible. Please help us all out by limiting the length of your introduction."

Use the space below to record alternative usage ideas.

Alternative Usage Ideas:

Idea 1. _____

Idea 2. _____

Alternative Usage Patter:

Patter 1. _____

_____

Patter 2. _____

_____

Family History

By Millbower and Yager

So, we moved again. This time. . .

Classroom Life—Introductions

The Cartoon: Flash Appearance

The Captioned Folder Name: FlashAp1

The Captionless Folder Name: FlashAp2

The Subject: Focusing on learning.

The Action: As the trainees watch, a trainer appears magically in a flash of light and a puff of smoke.

The Take: Instructors often feel the need to do something that captures attention at the start of a training session. This instructor does so through the use of magic.

The Use: As a vehicle for promising no "tricks," just learning, during the session.

The Patter: "Here's a drawing of a recent training event. As you can see, the participants were really impressed, but learning should be about knowledge, not gimmicks. Today, we'll focus on learning."

Use the space below to record alternative usage ideas.

Alternative Usage Ideas:

Idea 1. _____

Idea 2. _____

Alternative Usage Patter:

Patter 1. _____

_____

Patter 2. _____

_____

Flash Appearance

By Millbower and Yager

He's good!

Classroom Life—Introductions

The Cartoon: Unstated Objectives

The Captioned Folder Name: Unstate1

The Captionless Folder Name: Unstate2

The Subject: The varying objectives learners focus on in the classroom.

The Action: As the instructor is presenting the session objectives, the learners remember their own objectives.

The Take: Learners have very different needs and fears in a classroom, and instructors should be mindful of those needs.

The Use: To display learner emotions in a non-threatening manner.

The Patter: "I realize that we all have different objectives, some public and some private. Today, we will cover the stated course content, and hopefully, also help you meet your own objectives."

Use the space below to record alternative usage ideas.

Alternative Usage Ideas:

Idea 1. _____

Idea 2. _____

Alternative Usage Patter:

Patter 1. _____

_____

Patter 2. _____

_____

Unstated Objectives

By Millbower and Yager

Our objectives for today are . . .

Classroom Life—Expectations

The Cartoon: Boys with Toys

The Captioned Folder Name: Boy_Toy1

The Captionless Folder Name: Boy_Toy2

The Subject: Classroom etiquette.

The Action: One learner throws a tabletop toy. The toy bounces off the table, and strikes another learner in the ear.

The Take: Some people become so engrossed in the toys they have at hand that they forget where they are, and the etiquette of the learning room.

The Use: To remind learners that they should be respectful of the people around them.

The Patter: "On your table are some learning tools. Please feel free to use them, but please also be respectful of the people around you."

Use the space below to record alternative usage ideas.

Alternative Usage Ideas:

Idea 1. _____

Idea 2. _____

Alternative Usage Patter:

Patter 1. _____

_____

Patter 2. _____

_____

Boys with Toys

By Millbower and Yager

That's it! No more toys!!

Classroom Life—Expectations

The Cartoon: Cell Phone Etiquette

The Captioned Folder Name: Cellphn1

The Captionless Folder Name: Cellphn2

The Subject: Classroom etiquette.

The Action: A learner interrupts learning by talking on her cell phone.

The Take: People should not talk on cell phones during training events.

The Use: To remind learners that they should turn off their cell phones.

The Patter: "For the duration of this session, please respect the people around you and turn your cell phone off."

Use the space below to record alternative usage ideas.

Alternative Usage Ideas:

Idea 1. _____

Idea 2. _____

Alternative Usage Patter:

Patter 1. _____

_____

Patter 2. _____

_____

Cell Phone Etiquette

By Millbower and Yager

. . . and NO CELL PHONES!

Classroom Life—Expectations

The Cartoon: Learner Expectations

The Captioned Folder Name: Learner1

The Captionless Folder Name: Learner2

The Subject: The hidden expectations that learners have.

The Action: As an instructor seeks to determine learner expectations for the class, one participant shares her true expectation.

The Take: Learners often don't know enough about the content to be covered to have valid expectations, resulting in learner expectations that are fundamentally different from instructor expectations.

The Use: As a framework for guiding learner expectation discussions.

The Patter: "There are some expectations you may have that I cannot fulfill. Here might be one. Excluding going home early, what are some learning expectations you have from this class?"

Use the space below to record alternative usage ideas.

Alternative Usage Ideas:

Idea 1. _____

Idea 2. _____

Alternative Usage Patter:

Patter 1. _____

_____

Patter 2. _____

_____

Learner Expectations

By Millbower and Yager

We would like to go home early.

Classroom Life—Expectations

The Cartoon: Restroom Break

The Captioned Folder Name: Restrm1

The Captionless Folder Name: Restrm2

The Subject: Biological needs.

The Action: A learner struggles mightily to maintain his composure while nature calls.

The Take: Instructors talk about honoring their learners needs, and one of the most basic needs is the call of nature.

The Use: Display during a logistics discussion, as you give directions to the rest rooms.

The Patter: "In case you find yourself in this learner's situation, the restrooms are . . ."

Use the space below to record alternative usage ideas.

Alternative Usage Ideas:

Idea 1. _____

Idea 2. _____

Alternative Usage Patter:

Patter 1. _____

_____

Patter 2. _____

_____

Restroom Break

By Millbower and Yager

Does anyone need a break?

Classroom Life—Activities

The Cartoon: Peek-a-Boo

The Captioned Folder Name: Peekabo1

The Captionless Folder Name: Peekabo2

The Subject: Fear of losing control.

The Action: An instructor asks learners to close their eyes. When everyone has done so, the instructor makes a face at the unsuspecting learners.

The Take: Unspoken fears, such as the fear of a loss of control over the learning environment, prevent full learner participation in many activities.

The Use: To dispel unspoken fear when asking learners to participate in a "closed eye" activity.

The Patter: "In a minute, I'm going to ask you to close your eyes. I realize that this can be nerve-wracking for some people, so I've provided a drawing of what really happens when your eyes are closed."

Use the space below to record alternative usage ideas.

Alternative Usage Ideas:

Idea 1. _____

Idea 2. _____

Alternative Usage Patter:

Patter 1. _____

_____

Patter 2. _____

_____

Peek-a-boo

By Millbower and Yager

Now, please close your eyes.

Classroom Life—Activities

The Cartoon: Role-Play Extravaganza

The Captioned Folder Name: RolePly1

The Captionless Folder Name: RolePly2

The Subject: Overacting.

The Action: To stage a role-play, a classroom has been remade into a grand Hollywood movie set.

The Take: Participants sometimes worry about acting skills during role-plays. This is unfortunate because the learning comes not from the acting, but from the discussion that follows the role-play.

The Use: To dispel learner fears regarding their acting abilities.

The Patter: "Fortunately, our role-play will not be this extravagant. Remember, this isn't Hollywood, and there are no cameras present. Just have a good time with this activity, and focus on the learning."

Use the space below to record alternative usage ideas.

Alternative Usage Ideas:

Idea 1. _____

Idea 2. _____

Alternative Usage Patter:

Patter 1. _____

_____

Patter 2. _____

_____

Role-play Extravagenza

By Millbower and Yager

This is the last time I'll volunteer!

Classroom Life—Activities

The Cartoon: Titanic

The Captioned Folder Name: Titanic1

The Captionless Folder Name: Titanic2

The Subject: The unstated apprehension learners feel towards icebreakers.

The Action: As an instructor introduces an icebreaker, the learners visualize the class crashing into an iceberg, just like the Titanic.

The Take: Icebreakers can "sink" a class if presented improperly.

The Use: To minimize the negative aspects surrounding activities at the start of a learning event.

The Patter: "I can relate to the people in this cartoon. To me, pointless icebreakers are a waste of time. We will engage in learning activities, but at no time will we resort to cheap icebreaker tricks."

Use the space below to record alternative usage ideas.

Alternative Usage Ideas:

Idea 1. _____

Idea 2. _____

Alternative Usage Patter:

Patter 1. _____

_____

Patter 2. _____

_____

Titanic

By Millbower and Yager

Let's start with an ice breaker.

Classroom Life—Activities

The Cartoon: Trapeze

The Captioned Folder Name: Trapeze1

The Captionless Folder Name: Trapeze2

The Subject: Extravagant learning activities.

The Action: Two learners on a trapeze complain about the extravagant learning activities.

The Take: Not knowing what they are getting themselves into, learners are often afraid to volunteer for activities.

The Use: As a tool for acknowledging learner apprehension when seeking volunteers.

The Patter: "I need a volunteer, and, unlike the activity pictured in the cartoon, this activity will not 'get out of hand.' "

Use the space below to record alternative usage ideas.

Alternative Usage Ideas:

Idea 1.   _____

Idea 2.   _____

Alternative Usage Patter:

Patter 1.   _____

            _____

Patter 2.   _____

            _____

Trapeze

By Millbower and Yager

These activities are out of hand.

Classroom Life—Activities

The Cartoon: Volunteers

The Captioned Folder Name: Voluntr1

The Captionless Folder Name: Voluntr2

The Subject: Learner reluctance to volunteer for activities.

The Action: An instructor asks for volunteers while the learners look away.

The Take: Most learners are reluctant to volunteer because of their internal fears.

The Use: When asking for volunteers.

The Patter: "As you can see by this cartoon, people are sometimes reluctant to volunteer. Unfortunately, this next activity won't work unless I have some help. Would someone please volunteer? I promise there is no hidden catch."

Use the space below to record alternative usage ideas.

Alternative Usage Ideas:

Idea 1. _____

Idea 2. _____

Alternative Usage Patter:

Patter 1. _____

_____

Patter 2. _____

_____

Volunteers

By Millbower and Yager

Who'd like to assist me?

Classroom Life—Activities

The Cartoon: War Games

The Captioned Folder Name: WarGame1

The Captionless Folder Name: Wargame2

The Subject: Experiential learning.

The Action: Two soldiers sit in a foxhole as shells explode around them.

The Take: Sometimes, classroom competition generates hostility, especially when they take experiential learning activities too seriously.

The Use: As a disclaimer when learners are displaying aggressive behavior after an activity.

The Patter: "What we just did was an activity, not a conflict. If you feel any anxiety over it, please relax and come out of whatever 'foxhole' you may find yourself in."

Use the space below to record alternative usage ideas.

Alternative Usage Ideas:

Idea 1. _____

Idea 2. _____

Alternative Usage Patter:

Patter 1. _____

_____

Patter 2. _____

_____

War Games

By Millbower and Yager

I hate experiential learning.

Classroom Life—Activities

The Cartoon: Wrecked Room

The Captioned Folder Name: Wreckrm1

The Captionless Folder Name: Wreckrm2

The Subject: Establishing parameters for activity participation.

The Action: The learners have just completed an experiential learning activity that left the instructor, and the classroom, a complete mess.

The Take: Experiential activities need to have parameters to prevent degeneration into chaos.

The Use: To set up the guidelines for activities that involve the physical environment.

The Patter: "We want you to enjoy the next activity, but please remember that we only have this room for eight hours."

Use the space below to record alternative usage ideas.

Alternative Usage Ideas:

Idea 1. _____

Idea 2. _____

Alternative Usage Patter:

Patter 1. _____

_____

Patter 2. _____

_____

Wrecked Room

By Millbower and Yager

That was GREAT!!

Classroom Life—Breaks

The Cartoon: Asleep

The Captioned Folder Name: Asleep1

The Captionless Folder Name: Asleep2

The Subject: Overlong sessions.

The Action: When the instructor asks if anyone wants to take a break, there is no reply. The learners have already begun their break.

The Take: If a session continues beyond the learners' ability to focus, they will take their own break.

The Use: Instructors are vigilant in attending to their learners' needs for a break. Sometimes however, the subject matter, timing, or the biological clock is such that there is no choice but to continue until the segment ends. Use this cartoon to reconnect with your learners by displaying it as you call for a break.

The Patter: "I think we should call a break before we all end up like these people."

Use the space below to record alternative usage ideas.

Alternative Usage Ideas:

Idea 1. _____

Idea 2. _____

Alternative Usage Patter:

Patter 1. _____

_____

Patter 2. _____

_____

Asleep

By Millbower and Yager

Is anyone ready for a break?

Classroom Life—Breaks

The Cartoon: Overdue

The Captioned Folder Name: Overdue1

The Captionless Folder Name: Overdue2

The Subject: Lengthy learning segments.

The Action: Two learners are crawling, exhausted, out of a classroom.

The Take: Learning segments sometimes continue past a reasonable breaking point.

The Use: Display at the end of a lengthy learning segment as an acknowledgment that the segment was long, and the learners need a break.

The Patter: "Let's take a break now, before this happens to any of you."

Use the space below to record alternative usage ideas.

Alternative Usage Ideas:

Idea 1. _____

Idea 2. _____

Alternative Usage Patter:

Patter 1. _____

_____

Patter 2. _____

_____

Overdue

By Millbower and Yager

Finally, a break!

Classroom Life—Breaks

The Cartoon: Sentenced to Training

The Captioned Folder Name: SentTrn1

The Captionless Folder Name: SentTrn2

The Subject: Putting learners at ease.

The Action: A learner, imprisoned in a training room, talks to a loved one through the protective glass.

The Take: Learners often feel trapped, as if in prison, by training.

The Use: As an acknowledgment that some learners may have been required to attend learning.

The Patter: "Have you ever been 'sentenced' to training? It's happened to all of us. I can't give you a 'pardon,' but, if we laugh at the situation, our 'sentence' may be more enjoyable."

Use the space below to record alternative usage ideas.

Alternative Usage Ideas:

Idea 1. _____

Idea 2. _____

Alternative Usage Patter:

Patter 1. _____

_____

Patter 2. _____

_____

Sentenced to Training

By Millbower and Yager

How long are you in for?

Classroom Life—Food

The Cartoon: After the Rush

The Captioned Folder Name: AftRush1

The Captionless Folder Name: AftRush2

The Subject: Clean up responsibility.

The Action: The first panel presents a well-placed food display before learners enter the learning environment. The second panel displays the aftermath of the learner's entry into the classroom.

The Take: Food, when offered in a training setting, tends to be devoured quickly, leaving a clean up mess behind.

The Use: As a humorous reminder when you want learners to clean up after themselves.

The Patter: "We have provided breakfast for you. Please be considerate of our staff. As you can see in this cartoon, some groups are not."

Use the space below to record alternative usage ideas.

Alternative Usage Ideas:

Idea 1. _____

Idea 2. _____

Alternative Usage Patter:

Patter 1. _____

_____

Patter 2. _____

_____

After the Rush

By Millbower and Yager

Before   After

Classroom Life—Food

The Cartoon: Come and Get It

The Captioned Folder Name: ComeGet1

The Captionless Folder Name: ComeGet2

The Subject: Serving food in an orderly fashion.

The Action: An instructor holds out a plate of food and is quickly engulfed by learners.

The Take: Sometimes, food is so inviting that people crowd around to get their share. At moments like this, aggressive tendencies can emerge.

The Use: While inviting learners to help themselves to free food.

The Patter: "Please help yourself to some food; in an orderly manner . . . of course."

Use the space below to record alternative usage ideas.

Alternative Usage Ideas:

Idea 1. _____

Idea 2. _____

Alternative Usage Patter:

Patter 1. _____

_____

Patter 2. _____

_____

Come and Get It

By Millbower and Yager

Would anyone like a donut?

Classroom Life—Food

The Cartoon: Hunger Growl

The Captioned Folder Name: Hunger1

The Captionless Folder Name: Hunger2

The Subject: Hunger pains before lunch.

The Action: A learner's stomach growls so fiercely that the noise startles another learner.

The Take: Stomach growls betray the need for food.

The Use: As a vehicle for introducing the lunch break.

The Patter: "Is anyone ready for lunch?"

Use the space below to record alternative usage ideas.

Alternative Usage Ideas:

Idea 1. _____

Idea 2. _____

Alternative Usage Patter:

Patter 1. _____

_____

Patter 2. _____

_____

Hunger Growl

By Millbower and Yager

I guess it's time for lunch!

Classroom Life—Food

The Cartoon: Lunch Aftermath

The Captioned Folder Name: LunchAf1

The Captionless Folder Name: LunchAf2

The Subject: After lunch discomfort.

The Action: The learners, having overeaten, have returned from lunch.

The Take: After-lunch instruction can be difficult, especially when learners overeat.

The Use: To introduce the after-lunch session.

The Patter: "How was lunch? Hopefully, none of you feel as full as the people in this group. An after-lunch tiredness or discomfort is normal, regardless of how little you eat. If you feel the need to take a break, please say so, and we'll take one at the nearest possible breaking point."

Use the space below to record alternative usage ideas.

Alternative Usage Ideas:

Idea 1. _____

Idea 2. _____

Alternative Usage Patter:

Patter 1. _____

_____

Patter 2. _____

_____

Lunch Aftermath

By Millbower and Yager

Lunch must have been filling.

Classroom Life—Discussions

The Cartoon: Biker Sharing

The Captioned Folder Name: Biker1

The Captionless Folder Name: Biker2

The Subject: Paired discussions.

The Action: An instructor has asked each learner to share their emotions with their neighbor, to the dismay of one learner sitting next to a rough looking character.

The Take: People are often afraid to share their emotions in forced discussion situations.

The Use: As a tool for dissipating fear.

The Patter: "Next, I'd like you to share your reactions with your neighbor. Fortunately, no one here looks like this guy, so it should be safe to share."

Use the space below to record alternative usage ideas.

Alternative Usage Ideas:

Idea 1. _____

Idea 2. _____

Alternative Usage Patter:

Patter 1. _____

_____

Patter 2. _____

_____

Biker Sharing

By Millbower and Yager

Share your feelings with your neighbor.

Classroom Life—Discussions

The Cartoon: Blackboard Jungle

The Captioned Folder Name: Blkbrd1

The Captionless Folder Name: Blkbrd2

The Subject: Encouraging questions.

The Action: An instructor has completely lost his learners during the previous explanation.

The Take: Learners can become confused during lectures, but, due to a belief that asking for clarifications exposes ones limitations as a learner, are often reluctant to ask questions.

The Use: After a presentation of difficult material to relax the learners and encourage questions.

The Patter: "Sometimes, new information can be confusing. Maybe I'm not as clear as I might like, or the new concepts need more illumination. Are there any questions?"

Use the space below to record alternative usage ideas.

Alternative Usage Ideas:

Idea 1. _____

Idea 2. _____

Alternative Usage Patter:

Patter 1. _____

_____

Patter 2. _____

_____

Blackboard Jungle

By Millbower and Yager

Are there any questions?

Classroom Life—Discussions

The Cartoon: Stupid Questions

The Captioned Folder Name: Stupid?1

The Captionless Folder Name: Stupid?2

The Subject: Encouraging questions.

The Action: As a learner is asking a question, the instructor thinks that the question is stupid.

The Take: Learners fear that instructors might not be receptive to their questions, and as a result, do not ask.

The Use: As a preface to asking for learner questions.

The Patter: "An open and honest dialog is an important part of today's learnings. No question is stupid. I promise to never think like this. So today, please ask questions."

Use the space below to record alternative usage ideas.

Alternative Usage Ideas:

Idea 1. _____

Idea 2. _____

Alternative Usage Patter:

Patter 1. _____

_____

Patter 2. _____

_____

Stupid Questions

By Millbower and Yager

Thank you for asking.

Classroom Life—Evaluations

The Cartoon: Five out of Five

The Captioned Folder Name: FiveFiv1

The Captionless Folder Name: FiveFiv2

The Subject: Encouraging evaluation comments.

The Action: A participant rates a class highly because there was a long lunch period.

The Take: Bribery may gain improved evaluation scores, but provides little actionable information.

The Use: To frame evaluation comments expectations.

The Patter: "We need your help on these evaluations. Regardless of the length of our lunch, we need to know what you thought of the content of the class. Please give us details that will help us improve it for the next time."

Use the space below to record alternative usage ideas.

Alternative Usage Ideas:

Idea 1. _____

Idea 2. _____

Alternative Usage Patter:

Patter 1. _____

_____

Patter 2. _____

_____

Five out of Five

By Millbower and Yager

It's a "5." We got a long lunch.

Classroom Life—Tests and Evaluations

The Cartoon: Paper Trail

The Captioned Folder Name: Paper1

The Captionless Folder Name: Paper2

The Subject: Test instructions.

The Action: A learner, whose pockets are stuffed with notes, is reminded not to cheat.

The Take: Reminding learners not to cheat can be uncomfortable for instructors. This cartoon accomplishes the task without the embarrassment.

The Use: As a final reminder prior to the beginning of an exam.

The Patter: "And, as a reminder, no cheating!"

Use the space below to record alternative usage ideas.

Alternative Usage Ideas:

Idea 1. _____

Idea 2. _____

Alternative Usage Patter:

Patter 1. _____

_____

Patter 2. _____

_____

Paper Trail

By Millbower and Yager

And remember, NO CHEATING.

Classroom Life—Tests and Evaluations

The Cartoon: Three out of Five

The Captioned Folder Name: ThreeFi1

The Captionless Folder Name: ThreeFi2

The Subject: Encouraging evaluation comments.

The Action: A participant rates a class poorly because donuts were not served.

The Take: What instructional designers and instructors value is sometimes at odds with learner needs.

The Use: To frame evaluation comments expectations.

The Patter: "It is useful to know that donuts should have been served, but we would appreciate substantive detail on your evaluation form. Any comments you have will help us improve the next class and would be greatly appreciated."

Use the space below to record alternative usage ideas.

Alternative Usage Ideas:

Idea 1. _____

Idea 2. _____

Alternative Usage Patter:

Patter 1. _____

_____

Patter 2. _____

_____

Three out of Five

By Millbower and Yager

It's a "3." Next time serve donuts.

Classroom Life—Classroom Awards

The Cartoon: Best Class

The Captioned Folder Name: B_Class1

The Captionless Folder Name: B_Class2

The Subject: Instructor recognition.

The Action: The instructor recognizes the participants.

The Take: The completion of a course and an Academy Awards ceremony have some commonalities. This cartoon features an award that participants might give each other at the conclusion of a course, if they were allowed to do so. In this case, the instructor is acknowledging the participants.

The Use: As a celebration of learning and a humorous recognition of the participants.

The Patter: "An the award for the best class goes to . . . you!"

Use the space below to record alternative usage ideas.

Alternative Usage Ideas:

Idea 1. _____

Idea 2. _____

Alternative Usage Patter:

Patter 1. _____

_____

Patter 2. _____

_____

Best Class

By Millbower and Yager

The best class award goes to us!

Classroom Life—Classroom Awards

The Cartoon: Longest Nap

The Captioned Folder Name: LongNap1

The Captionless Folder Name: LongNap2

The Subject: Participant recognition.

The Action: The learners recognize the person who slept the most during the course.

The Take: The completion of a course and an Academy Awards ceremony have some commonalities. This cartoon features an award that participants might give each other at the conclusion of a course, if they were allowed to do so. In this case, the participants are acknowledging the learner who catnapped while others learned.

The Use: As a celebration of learning and a humorous recognition of various learners.

The Patter: "An the award for the longest nap goes to . . ."

Use the space below to record alternative usage ideas.

Alternative Usage Ideas:

Idea 1. _____

Idea 2. _____

Alternative Usage Patter:

Patter 1. _____

_____

Patter 2. _____

_____

Longest Nap

By Millbower and Yager

The longest nap award goes to . .

Classroom Life—Classroom Awards

The Cartoon: Most Donuts

The Captioned Folder Name: M_Donut1

The Captionless Folder Name: M_Donut2

The Subject: Participant recognition.

The Action: The learners recognize the person who ate the most food during the course.

The Take: The completion of a course and an Academy Awards ceremony have some commonalities. This cartoon features an award that participants might give each other at the conclusion of a course, if they were allowed to do so. In this case, the participants are acknowledging the learner who ate more than the other participants.

The Use: As a celebration of learning and a humorous recognition of various learners

The Patter: "An the award for the most food consumed goes to . . ."

Use the space below to record alternative usage ideas.

Alternative Usage Ideas:

Idea 1.   _____

Idea 2.   _____

Alternative Usage Patter:

Patter 1. _____

           _____

Patter 2. _____

           _____

Most Dounts

By Millbower and Yager

© 2002, Stylus Publishing, LLC.

The most donuts eaten
award goes to . . .

Classroom Life—Classroom Awards

The Cartoon: Most Questions

The Captioned Folder Name: M_Quest1

The Captionless Folder Name: M_Quest2

The Subject: Participant recognition.

The Action: The learners recognize the person who asked the most questions during the course.

The Take: The completion of a course and an Academy Awards ceremony have some commonalities. This cartoon features an award that participants might give each other at the conclusion of a course, if they were allowed to do so. In this case, the participants are acknowledging the learner who asked more questions than the rest of the participants.

The Use: As a celebration of learning and a humorous recognition of various learners.

The Patter: "An the award for the most questions asked goes to . . ."

Use the space below to record alternative usage ideas.

Alternative Usage Ideas:

Idea 1. _____

Idea 2. _____

Alternative Usage Patter:

Patter 1. _____

_____

Patter 2. _____

_____

Most Questions

By Millbower and Yager

The award for the most questions asked goes to . . .

Classroom Life—Conclusions

The Cartoon: Bad News

The Captioned Folder Name: BadNews1

The Captionless Folder Name: BadNews2

The Subject: The conclusion of a successful course.

The Action: Learners tearfully react to the end of a course.

The Take: Some courses are so successful that people react with sadness to the end of the course.

The Use: At the conclusion of a course. In situations where people have bonded with each other, use it to honor unstated emotions. In situations where people have not felt emotional connections, use it in a kidding manner.

The Patter: "At this time, I have very sad news for you; our time together is at an end. Now, I realize that some of you may react with great sorrow, but remember, you made new friends and learned a great deal."

Use the space below to record alternative usage ideas.

Alternative Usage Ideas:

Idea 1. _____

Idea 2. _____

Alternative Usage Patter:

Patter 1. _____

_____

Patter 2. _____

_____

Bad News

By Millbower and Yager

I'm sorry to say our class is over.

Classroom Life—Conclusions

The Cartoon: Blah, Blah, Blah

The Captioned Folder Name: Blah1

The Captionless Folder Name: Blah2

The Subject: Overly talkative instructors.

The Action: The instructor continues to drone on, even though the learners have lost interest.

The Take: Instructors sometimes like to discuss every facet of a subject, where learners only need to comprehend the big picture. Unfortunately, learners rarely verbalize these needs.

The Use: When an instructor realizes that the lecture was long winded.

The Patter: "I think I'll conclude now, before you begin reacting like these people."

Use the space below to record alternative usage ideas.

Alternative Usage Ideas:

Idea 1. _____

Idea 2. _____

Alternative Usage Patter:

Patter 1. _____

_____

Patter 2. _____

_____

Blah, Blah, Blah

By Millbower and Yager

. . . and another point . . .

Classroom Life—Conclusions

The Cartoon: Hat Toss

The Captioned Folder Name: HatToss1

The Captionless Folder Name: HatToss2

The Subject: Graduation ceremonies.

The Action: The learners toss their hats in the air to celebrate completion of the course.

The Take: Completion of a course is a cause for celebration and should be honored.

The Use: At the end of the course content, to set up graduation ceremony.

The Patter: "We've almost completed this course. But before we end, we have one item left . . . GRADUATION!"

Use the space below to record alternative usage ideas.

Alternative Usage Ideas:

Idea 1. _____

Idea 2. _____

Alternative Usage Patter:

Patter 1. _____

_____

Patter 2. _____

_____

Hat Toss

By Millbower and Yager

YEAHHH! WE DID IT!

Classroom Life—Conclusions

The Cartoon: High Fives

The Captioned Folder Name: HighFiv1

The Captionless Folder Name: HighFiv2

The Subject: Celebrating the conclusion of an activity, competition, or a course.

The Action: The learners are engaging in sports-related celebrations.

The Take: The adrenaline rush that accompanies the completion of an activity, competition, or a course is similar to the emotion that occurs at sporting events.

The Use: To encourage a feeling of accomplishment.

The Patter: "We did it! You were great! These people think so, too!"

Use the space below to record alternative usage ideas.

Alternative Usage Ideas:

Idea 1. _____

Idea 2. _____

Alternative Usage Patter:

Patter 1. _____

_____

Patter 2. _____

_____

High Fives

By Millbower and Yager

YESSSSSSS!

Classroom Life—Conclusions

The Cartoon: Night of the Learning Dead

The Captioned Folder Name: Nightof1

The Captionless Folder Name: Nightof2

The Subject: Focusing on the positive results of a learning experience.

The Action: The learners are leaving the learning environment in a trance.

The Take: Learning can sometimes be a mind-numbing experience.

The Use: As an acknowledgment that the learners may be numb from information overload.

The Patter: "It can be difficult to absorb the vast amount of information presented during training. As you leave today, you may feel 'brain dead.' As you reflect on the information you absorbed today, I would also encourage you to realize how much you have accomplished."

Use the space below to record alternative usage ideas.

Alternative Usage Ideas:

Idea 1. _____

Idea 2. _____

Alternative Usage Patter:

Patter 1. _____

_____

Patter 2. _____

_____

Night of the Learning Dead

By Millbower and Yager

Good night. Have a great evening!

Classroom Life—Conclusions

The Cartoon: Over It

The Captioned Folder Name: Over_It1

The Captionless Folder Name: Over_It2

The Subject: Orderly exits from the learning environment.

The Action: The instructor has ended the segment or class, and the overly anxious learners have responding by running toward the door.

The Take: Learners sometimes feel trapped in the classroom environment and can't wait to leave.

The Use: As a humorous acknowledgment that learners may want to exit the learning environment as soon as possible.

The Patter: "It's been a long day, and we've accomplished a great deal. Now, some of you look anxious to be on your way. Let's end now, before that anxiousness turns into a stampede."

Use the space below to record alternative usage ideas.

Alternative Usage Ideas:

Idea 1. _____

Idea 2. _____

Alternative Usage Patter:

Patter 1. _____

_____

Patter 2. _____

_____

Over It

By Millbower and Yager

You're free to go. Thanks for . . .

Classroom Life—Conclusions

The Cartoon: Past Time

The Captioned Folder Name: PstTime1

The Captionless Folder Name: PstTime2

The Subject: Classes that continue past their slated end time.

The Action: The instructor is concluding her remarks, after having run past the scheduled end time.

The Take: Instructors should never continue a class past the scheduled end time.

The Use: To conclude a course in a timely fashion.

The Patter: "We could discuss this subject all day, but our scheduled end time is almost here, and I want to honor your time. Let's conclude now."

Use the space below to record alternative usage ideas.

Alternative Usage Ideas:

Idea 1. _____

Idea 2. _____

Alternative Usage Patter:

Patter 1. _____

_____

Patter 2. _____

_____

Past Time

By Millbower and Yager

. . . and in conclusion . . .

Classroom Life—Conclusions

The Cartoon: Triple Ending

The Captioned Folder Name: TripEnd1

The Captionless Folder Name: TripEnd2

The Subject: The conclusion of a course.

The Action: This cartoon displays a backside shot of the learners.

The Take: Everything has an end.

The Use: To conclude a course.

The Patter: "Thank you all for attending today. This truly is THE END."

Use the space below to record alternative usage ideas.

Alternative Usage Ideas:

Idea 1. _____

Idea 2. _____

Alternative Usage Patter:

Patter 1. _____

_____

Patter 2. _____

_____

Triple Ending

By Millbower and Yager

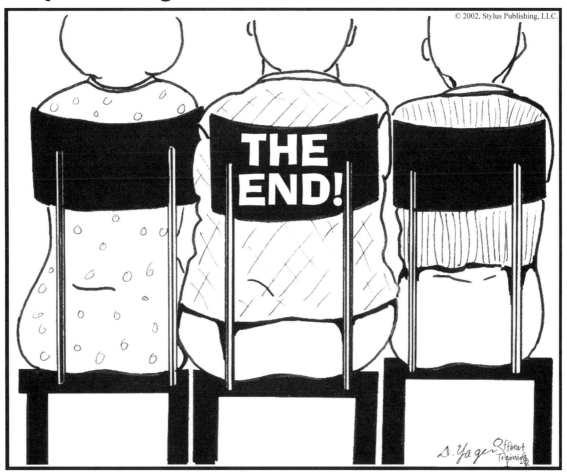

Class over. No ifs, ands, or buts!

Part Two

By Millbower and Yager

"Because humor often depends on small details, people pay close attention to a message in which they are looking for humor." —John Merell, Ph.D. (1997), *Humor Works*. Amherst, MA: HRD Press, Inc.

Training Topics—Brainstorming/Creativity

The Cartoon: Neanderthal Brainstorming

The Captioned Folder Name: Neander1

The Captionless Folder Name: Neander2

The Subject: Accepting new ideas.

The Action: A clan of Neanderthals is gathered around a fireplace trying to figure out a way to ignite the fire. One member of the clan discovers a solution, but the clan's most vocal member dismisses the idea before it can be tried.

The Take: Acceptance of ideas is a critical component of brainstorming activities. One never knows where the next great idea will come from.

The Use: To establish a framework for a brainstorming activity.

The Patter: "You may have wondered what happened to the Neanderthals; why they did not survive. Recent research suggests that they lacked the ability to brainstorm successfully. As we brainstorm, remember the Neanderthals and fully explore all the ideas presented. Don't become a Neanderthal yourself!"

Use the space below to record alternative usage ideas.

Alternative Usage Ideas:

Idea 1. _____

Idea 2. _____

Alternative Usage Patter:

Patter 1. _____

_____

Patter 2. _____

_____

Neanderthal Brainstorming By Millbower and Yager

Rubbing sticks? What a stupid idea!

Training Topics—Career Development

The Cartoon: Career Evolution

The Captioned Folder Name: Career1

The Captionless Folder Name: Career2

The Subject: Envisioning the future.

The Action: Two fish are looking at the shore, daydreaming about evolving into higher order beings.

The Take: Careers go through evolutions that may at times seem as slow as evolution itself.

The Use: As a framework to aid participants in envisioning the future.

The Patter: "Evolution can be painfully slow, but it can happen. These fish had no control over their evolution, but you can exert influence over yours. What do you want to evolve into?"

Use the space below to record alternative usage ideas.

Alternative Usage Ideas:

Idea 1. _____

Idea 2. _____

Alternative Usage Patter:

Patter 1. _____

_____

Patter 2. _____

_____

Career Evolution

By Millbower and Yager

I hope I evolve into a human.

Training Topics—Career Development

The Cartoon: Try to Fly

The Captioned Folder Name: Try_Fly1

The Captionless Folder Name: Try_Fly2

The Subject: Venturing into the unknown.

The Action: A baby bird would like to venture out into the world, but is afraid to fly.

The Take: Jumping into the unknown can be frightening, but is essential to future success.

The Use: As an example of the need for courage when planning career moves.

The Patter: "It is much easier to be comfortable in your current circumstance than it is to try something new. Jumping into the unknown can be very frightening. Sometimes though, you just have to trust your abilities and spread your wings."

Use the space below to record alternative usage ideas.

Alternative Usage Ideas:

Idea 1. _____

Idea 2. _____

Alternative Usage Patter:

Patter 1. _____

_____

Patter 2. _____

_____

Try to Fly

By Millbower and Yager

You'll never fly unless you try.

Training Topics—Change

The Cartoon: *Change Comes Calling*

The Captioned Folder Name: *Change1*

The Captionless Folder Name: *Change2*

The Subject: The fear of change.

The Action: Change, in the form of a shadow, is knocking on the door, as the people inside try to ignore it.

The Take: Change is unavoidable. Welcome it when it arrives.

The Use: During a coping-with-change discussion.

The Patter: "Everyone is afraid of change. But when change 'knocks on the door,' you have to answer it. Ignoring change will not make it go away."

Use the space below to record alternative usage ideas.

Alternative Usage Ideas:

Idea 1. _____

Idea 2. _____

Alternative Usage Patter:

Patter 1. _____

_____

Patter 2. _____

_____

Change Comes Calling

By Millbower and Yager

I tried ignoring it. It won't leave!

Training Topics—Change

The Cartoon: Flavor of the Month

The Captioned Folder Name: Flavor1

The Captionless Folder Name: Flavor2

The Subject: Frequent management initiatives.

The Action: A management ice cream parlor sells the 'flavor of the month.'

The Take: Employees often approach new management initiatives skeptically, regarding them as successive fads.

The Use: To acknowledge employee skepticism and diffuse it with humor.

The Patter: "I realize that some people regard new initiatives as 'flavors of the month.' To be clear, this is not one of those. We have given this initiative a great deal of thought and intend to maintain it by . . ."

Use the space below to record alternative usage ideas.

Alternative Usage Ideas:

Idea 1. _____

Idea 2. _____

Alternative Usage Patter:

Patter 1. _____

_____

Patter 2. _____

_____

Flavor of the Month

By Millbower and Yager

Do you think they'll buy it?

Training Topics—Communication Skills

The Cartoon: What Polly Wants

The Captioned Folder Name: WhatPol1

The Captionless Folder Name: WhatPol2

The Subject: Miscommunication challenges.

The Action: Polly has asked for a cracker, and instead discovers that she has been given a computer "hacker."

The Take: Small miscommunications can lead to huge mistakes, even when the intended communication appears obvious to the sender.

The Use: As an example of the need for clear communication from the sender to the receiver, and back to the sender.

The Patter: "To us, it should be obvious that what Polly would want is a cracker, not a hacker. In this case, it was not obvious to the receiver of the message. This illustrates the importance of verifying the meaning of a communication before you respond. Small miscommunications can lead to huge mistakes."

Use the space below to record alternative usage ideas.

Alternative Usage Ideas:

Idea 1. _____

Idea 2. _____

Alternative Usage Patter:

Patter 1. _____

_____

Patter 2. _____

_____

What Polly Wants

By Millbower and Yager

Polly want cracker, not HACKER!

Training Topics—Computer Based Training

The Cartoon: Simulations

The Captioned Folder Name: Simulat1

The Captionless Folder Name: Simulat2

The Subject: CBT realism.

The Action: A learner is ducking as a missile emerges from the computer screen.

The Take: Simulations have become pretty realistic.

The Use: As an introduction to a new simulation.

The Patter: "Our simulation is pretty realistic, but I promise, nothing will charge out of the screen at you."

Use the space below to record alternative usage ideas.

Alternative Usage Ideas:

Idea 1. _____

Idea 2. _____

Alternative Usage Patter:

Patter 1. _____

_____

Patter 2. _____

_____

Simulations

By Millbower and Yager

Wow! That's realistic!!

Training Topics—Computer Based Training

The Cartoon: Smoke Signals

The Captioned Folder Name: Smoke1

The Captionless Folder Name: Smoke2

The Subject: Distance learning.

The Action: Native American students are participating in distance learning by observing smoke signals in the distance.

The Take: Although technology has made communication easier, people have communicated over distances for years.

The Use: As a fun introduction to distance learning.

The Patter: "We tend to think of distance learning as a recent phenomena, but in reality, people have learned from a distance for years."

Use the space below to record alternative usage ideas.

Alternative Usage Ideas:

Idea 1. _____

Idea 2. _____

Alternative Usage Patter:

Patter 1. _____

_____

Patter 2. _____

_____

Smoke Signals

By Millbower and Yager

We're almost done downloading.

Training Topics—Conflict

The Cartoon: Mugged

The Captioned Folder Name: Mugged1

The Captionless Folder Name: Mugged2

The Subject: The emotion instructors feel after training sessions.

The Action: An instructor stumbles from the training room, exhausted from the session.

The Take: Instructors take their jobs so seriously, that sometimes, especially after mentally challenging sessions, they feel like they have been physically pummeled.

The Use: When a session becomes too intense, display this cartoon as a reminder that instructors are people too.

The Patter: "I'm sensing some hostility here. Please tell me, what can we do together to insure that today won't end like this?"

Use the space below to record alternative usage ideas.

Alternative Usage Ideas:

Idea 1. _____

Idea 2. _____

Alternative Usage Patter:

Patter 1. _____

_____

Patter 2. _____

_____

Mugged

By Millbower and Yager

That was a tough group!

Training Topics—Conflict

The Cartoon: Trainer Bodyguards

The Captioned Folder Name: TnrBody1

The Captionless Folder Name: TnrBody2

The Subject: Hostility.

The Action: An instructor enters the classroom, surrounded by bodyguards.

The Take: Instructors sometimes feel hostility from participants.

The Use: To set classroom discussion boundaries for difficult topics.

The Patter: "Our topic is sometimes difficult to discuss. It often generates a range of emotions, some of them negative. As we discuss this topic, remember that we are all in this together. No one should feel threatened by the discussion."

Use the space below to record alternative usage ideas.

Alternative Usage Ideas:

Idea 1. _____

Idea 2. _____

Alternative Usage Patter:

Patter 1. _____

_____

Patter 2. _____

_____

Trainer Bodyguards

By Millbower and Yager

Yesterday must have been rough.

Training Topics—Customer Service

The Cartoon: Canine Service Standards

The Captioned Folder Name: Canine1

The Captionless Folder Name: Canine2

The Subject: Customer service standards.

The Action: A dog instructor is reminding dog learners of the canine service standards.

The Take: What if dogs regarded humans as customers? This cartoon codifies doggie behavior into measurable behaviors.

The Use: To introduce customer service standards.

The Patter: "Everyone wants to feel welcomed when they contact a business. Our job is to make sure we approach them in a manner they expect."

Use the space below to record alternative usage ideas.

Alternative Usage Ideas:

Idea 1. _____

Idea 2. _____

Alternative Usage Patter:

Patter 1. _____

_____

Patter 2. _____

_____

Canine Service Standards By Millbower and Yager

Bark immediately, approach in 5 seconds, wag tail in 10.

Training Topics—Diversity

The Cartoon: Cave Conflict

The Captioned Folder Name: CaveCon1

The Captionless Folder Name: CaveCon2

The Subject: The consequences of ignoring people who are different.

The Action: A Neanderthal and a human have had an argument. In response, an instructor tries to encourage cooperation between them.

The Take: No one knows how Neanderthals and humans responded to each other. It would be unfortunate if knowledge was lost as a result of this lack of cooperation.

The Use: To encourage learners to listen to opinions different than their own.

The Patter: "How many Neanderthals do you know? . . . I mean REAL Neanderthals? Wouldn't it have been nice to know what they thought before they became extinct? You never know how long anyone has on this earth, so value every perspective you can get."

Use the space below to record alternative usage ideas.

Alternative Usage Ideas:

Idea 1. _____

Idea 2. _____

Alternative Usage Patter:

Patter 1. _____

_____

Patter 2. _____

_____

Cave Conflict

By Millbower and Yager

Can't you two just get along?!

Training Topics—Diversity

The Cartoon: Hades Angel

The Captioned Folder Name: Hades1

The Captionless Folder Name: Hades2

The Subject: The dangers inherent in shunning a person who acts differently.

The Action: The devil is inspecting his troops and bemoaning the fact that the angel in the group does not conform to group norms.

The Take: Sometimes, the non-conformist is in the right, and should not be chastised for being different.

The Use: To showcase the value of a minority perspective.

The Patter: "Have you ever felt like an angel amongst devils? We all do at times. Just because a person is in the minority, doesn't mean that their perspective is less valid."

Use the space below to record alternative usage ideas.

Alternative Usage Ideas:

Idea 1. _____

Idea 2. _____

Alternative Usage Patter:

Patter 1. _____

_____

Patter 2. _____

_____

Hades Angel

By Millbower and Yager

Why do you have to be different?

Training Topics—Diversity

The Cartoon: Mimes of the West

The Captioned Folder Name: Mimes1

The Captionless Folder Name: Mimes2

The Subject: Cultural differences.

The Action: A sheriff runs a mime out of town.

The Take: People sometimes react negatively to those they don't understand, irregardless of the strangers' abilities to enrich their lives.

The Use: During a diversity training, as a demonstration of culture clash.

The Patter: "Don't automatically chase away people who are different. You never know what the 'mime' has to say."

Use the space below to record alternative usage ideas.

Alternative Usage Ideas:

Idea 1. _____

Idea 2. _____

Alternative Usage Patter:

Patter 1. _____

_____

Patter 2. _____

_____

Mimes of the West

By Millbower and Yager

Your kind ain't welcome in this town.

Training Topics—Fiscal Awareness

The Cartoon: Bread and Water

The Captioned Folder Name: Bread1

The Captionless Folder Name: Bread2

The Subject: Placing budget cuts in perspective.

The Action: Two learners approach a buffet spread of bread and water.

The Take: Corporate belt tightening is rarely as terrible as it seems. No one is forced on a diet of bread and water.

The Use: To place budget cuts in their proper perspective.

The Patter: "I realize that budget cuts can be painful, but fortunately, our financial situation hasn't sunk this low."

Use the space below to record alternative usage ideas.

Alternative Usage Ideas:

Idea 1. _____

Idea 2. _____

Alternative Usage Patter:

Patter 1. _____

_____

Patter 2. _____

_____

Bread and Water

By Millbower and Yager

These budget cuts are extreme!

Training Topics:—Fiscal Awareness

The Cartoon: Pass the Plate

The Captioned Folder Name: PassPlt1

The Captionless Folder Name: PassPlt2

The Subject: Placing budget cuts in perspective.

The Action: During a class, a collection plate is being passed to collect money for the training department budget.

The Take: As tight as the budget gets, no one is passing the collection plate. The employees still get paid.

The Use: As a reminder that, even with budget cutting, things could be worse.

The Patter: "The budget may seem tight to you, but remember, we are all still being paid. No one is passing the plate."

Use the space below to record alternative usage ideas.

Alternative Usage Ideas:

Idea 1.   _____

Idea 2.   _____

Alternative Usage Patter:

Patter 1. _____

           _____

Patter 2. _____

           _____

Pass the Plate

By Millbower and Yager

The budget is tight this year.

Training Topics—HazCom

The Cartoon: Witches Brew

The Captioned Folder Name: Witches1

The Captionless Folder Name: Witches2

The Subject: Following directions.

The Action: Three witches are mixing a concoction in their cauldron when the wrong ingredient conjures up unexpected results.

The Take: Mixing chemicals improperly can lead to dangerous unintended side effects.

The Use: To demonstrate the importance of mixing the right chemicals in the correct amounts.

The Patter: "Here is a situation where mixing the wrong ingredients created a very unexpected result. Fortunately, no one was hurt, but mixing chemicals improperly is very dangerous."

Use the space below to record alternative usage ideas.

Alternative Usage Ideas:

Idea 1. _____

Idea 2. _____

Alternative Usage Patter:

Patter 1. _____

_____

Patter 2. _____

_____

Witches Brew

By Millbower and Yager

I said, "Turkish crown," not CIRCUS CLOWN!!!

Training Topics—Heavy Machinery Training

The Cartoon: Boulder Handling Tips

The Captioned Folder Name: Boulder1

The Captionless Folder Name: Boulder2

The Subject: Heavy machinery handling.

The Action: As part of his training regimen, a caveman is running downhill in front of a rolling boulder.

The Take: Any piece of heavy equipment can be dangerous if used improperly.

The Use: Immediately prior to practicing with the machinery.

The Patter: "Next, we're going to learn how to use the equipment. Knowing how to control the machinery leads to safety. Run the machinery; don't let it run you."

Use the space below to record alternative usage ideas.

Alternative Usage Ideas:

Idea 1. _____

Idea 2. _____

Alternative Usage Patter:

Patter 1. _____

_____

Patter 2. _____

_____

Boulder Handling Tips

By Millbower and Yager

Run Grog, run!

Training Topics—Management Theory

The Cartoon: Theory vs. Reality

The Captioned Folder Name: Theory1

The Captionless Folder Name: Theory2

The Subject: Placing theory in context.

The Action: A firing squad captain, studied in management theory, gets the firing squad command sequence wrong, with disastrous consequences.

The Take: What sounds good in theory, doesn't always prove effective in real life.

The Use: As a reminder for management trainees that the application of management theory affects lives, and must be used appropriately.

The Patter: "We have shared several useful theories today, but remember, that what you do in the workplace affects people. Be careful to apply these techniques appropriately. Otherwise, you might 'shoot yourself in the foot.'"

Use the space below to record alternative usage ideas.

Alternative Usage Ideas:

Idea 1. _____

Idea 2. _____

Alternative Usage Patter:

Patter 1. _____

_____

Patter 2. _____

_____

Theory vs. Reality

By Millbower and Yager

Ready . . . Fire . . . AIM!

Training Topics—Motivation

The Cartoon: Genghis Can't

The Captioned Folder Name: Genghis1

The Captionless Folder Name: Genghis2

The Subject: The cost of intimidation.

The Action: Genghis Khan practices motivation as only he could, by intimidation.

The Take: A leader may be able to command action through intimidation, but a "take no prisoners" approach leaves a wake of carnage behind.

The Use: As a demonstration of the ineffectiveness of intimidation in leadership situations.

The Patter: "You may be able to intimidate people to do your will, but the cost in personnel will be high. You may, in the process, 'kill' the spirit of your employees."

Use the space below to record alternative usage ideas.

Alternative Usage Ideas:

Idea 1. _____

Idea 2. _____

Alternative Usage Patter:

Patter 1. _____

_____

Patter 2. _____

_____

Genghis Can't

By Millbower and Yager

You're in charge now.

Training Topics—On-the-Job Training

The Cartoon: OJT in the Old West

The Captioned Folder Name: OJTWest1

The Captionless Folder Name: OJTWest2

The Subject: The learning process.

The Action: A western sheriff is training a new deputy, who is having difficulty remembering the gun fighting narration.

The Take: Regardless of the location and function, learning a new job can be difficult.

The Use: To help new trainees relax through the realization that every trainee has difficulty remembering critical information.

The Patter: "As you begin learning this new task, remember that every job presents learning difficulties at first. When you're learning, it's all right to 'sketch' when you should 'draw.' "

Use the space below to record alternative usage ideas.

Alternative Usage Ideas:

Idea 1. _____

Idea 2. _____

Alternative Usage Patter:

Patter 1. _____

_____

Patter 2. _____

_____

OJT in the old West.

By Millbower and Yager

Sketch? SKETCH!? No Bart.
It's ready, aim, DRAW!!

Training Topics—On-the-Job Training

The Cartoon: Revolutionary French OJT

The Captioned Folder Name: Rev_OJT1

The Captionless Folder Name: Rev_OJT2

The Subject: Performing tasks safely.

The Action: After an initial disastrous failure, a trainee tries again to safely operate a guillotine.

The Take: Regardless of the location and function, learning a new job can be dangerous.

The Use: As a reminder to new trainees to think and act safely when learning new tasks.

The Patter: "As you learn how to perform your new job, please be careful. At all times, think safety. Remember 'to move your hand first.' "

Use the space below to record alternative usage ideas.

Alternative Usage Ideas:

Idea 1. _____

Idea 2. _____

Alternative Usage Patter:

Patter 1. _____

_____

Patter 2. _____

_____

Revolutionary French OJT

By Millbower and Yager

Let's try it again. Only this time, remove your hand first!

Training Topics—Orientation

The Cartoon: Castaway Orientation

The Captioned Folder Name: Castawy1

The Captionless Folder Name: Castawy2

The Subject: Location familiarization.

The Action: A shipwreck survivor has just washed ashore onto a tropical island. The only resident of the island is so glad to see the stranger that he conducts a location orientation.

The Take: Orientation tours often point out the obvious, but are a necessary part of the introduction to any organization.

The Use: As an introduction to a site tour.

The Patter: "Our location is a little larger than this island. We have several areas to show you, so, if you're ready, let's show you our 'palm trees.' "

Use the space below to record alternative usage ideas.

Alternative Usage Ideas:

Idea 1. _____

Idea 2. _____

Alternative Usage Patter:

Patter 1. _____

_____

Patter 2. _____

_____

Castaway Orientation

By Millbower and Yager

. . . and here is our palm tree!

Training Topics—Safety Awareness

The Cartoon: Left Hook

The Captioned Folder Name: Left_Hk1

The Captionless Folder Name: Left_Hk2

The Subject: Maintaining a focus on safety.

The Action: A pirate salutes his captain with the wrong hand, clunking his head with his left hook.

The Take: Any procedure, if followed incorrectly, can lead to injury.

The Use: As a reminder that safety problems can occur when performing the simplest tasks.

The Patter: "Safety concerns can crop up in the least likely places. As you go about your daily activities, be careful. You never know when you'll get thrown a 'left hook.' "

Use the space below to record alternative usage ideas.

Alternative Usage Ideas:

Idea 1. _____

Idea 2. _____

Alternative Usage Patter:

Patter 1. _____

_____

Patter 2. _____

_____

Left Hook

By Millbower and Yager

Stupid. Use your RIGHT hand!

Training Topics—Sexual Harassment

The Cartoon: Fig Leaf

The Captioned Folder Name: FigLeaf1

The Captionless Folder Name: FigLeaf2

The Subject: The consequences of sexual harassment.

The Action: An angel, in the Garden of Eden, is explaining the need for fig leaves to Adam and Eve.

The Take: Sexual tension is as old as time itself. As the biblical Garden of Eden story demonstrates, the consequences of harassment can be severe.

The Use: As an introduction to sexual harassment issues.

The Patter: "You might think that sexual harassment is a new phenomena, but it's not. As people, we have struggled with this issue for ages. It is only recently that the law has been codified to define inappropriate behaviors. I'd like to discuss those laws with you . . ."

Use the space below to record alternative usage ideas.

Alternative Usage Ideas:

Idea 1. _____

Idea 2. _____

Alternative Usage Patter:

Patter 1. _____

_____

Patter 2. _____

_____

Fig Leaf

By Millbower and Yager

Are there any questions?

Training Topics—Sexual Harassment

The Cartoon: Peacock Strut

The Captioned Folder Name: Peacock1

The Captionless Folder Name: Peacock2

The Subject: Inappropriate behavior.

The Action: A male peacock is displaying his feathers to a non-appreciative female peacock audience.

The Take: Displays of virility may be a natural phenomena, but, unlike animals, humans can control their sexuality.

The Use: To, in a humorous fashion, begin a discussion of inappropriate behavior in the work environment.

The Patter: "This peacock got into trouble for inappropriate workplace behavior. What kind of behavior would you think the law lists as inappropriate workplace behavior for humans?"

Use the space below to record alternative usage ideas.

Alternative Usage Ideas:

Idea 1. _____

Idea 2. _____

Alternative Usage Patter:

Patter 1. _____

_____

Patter 2. _____

_____

Peacock Strut

By Millbower and Yager

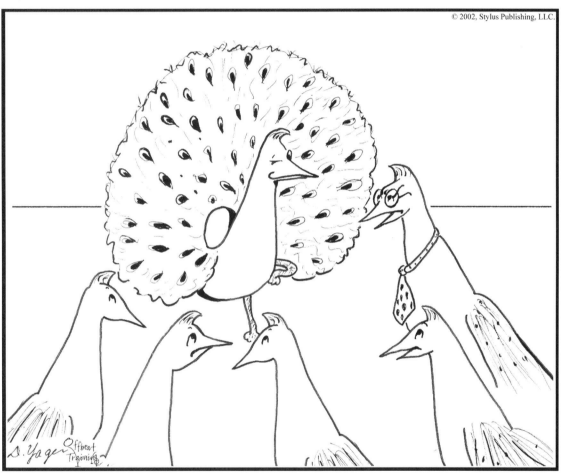

. . . and no open plumes at work.

Training Topics—Speech/Presentations

The Cartoon: Before-During-After

The Captioned Folder Name: Before1

The Captionless Folder Name: Before2

The Subject: A typical day in a presenter's life.

The Action: A presenter frantically sets up, presents, and collapses in exhaustion after the session ends.

The Take: The three stages of a presentation are normal and should be expected.

The Use: To display the emotions presenters experience.

The Patter: "All presenters experience these steps. Recognize that they are normal occurrences in classroom life. The key is to stay composed until the event is over."

Use the space below to record alternative usage ideas.

Alternative Usage Ideas:

Idea 1. _____

Idea 2. _____

Alternative Usage Patter:

Patter 1. _____

_____

Patter 2. _____

_____

Before-During-After

By Millbower and Yager

Whew!!

Training Topics—Speech/Presentations

The Cartoon: Blinded

The Captioned Folder Name: Blinded1

The Captionless Folder Name: Blinded2

The Subject: Overhead projector usage.

The Action: A novice presenter discovers, the hard way, that the overhead projector works.

The Take: Even simple technology can disrupt a presentation.

The Use: As a reminder of proper overhead projector usage.

The Patter: "Insure that you have checked all of your equipment, even the simple pieces. One failure can make you look like an amateur."

Use the space below to record alternative usage ideas.

Alternative Usage Ideas:

Idea 1. _____

Idea 2. _____

Alternative Usage Patter:

Patter 1. _____

_____

Patter 2. _____

_____

Blinded

By Millbower and Yager

Looks like we've got a rookie.

Training Topics—Speech/Presentations

The Cartoon: Pillow Talk

The Captioned Folder Name: Pillow1

The Captionless Folder Name: Pillow2

The Subject: Boring presentations.

The Action: A learner walks into the training room carrying a pillow because she knows that the presenter's boring style will put her to sleep.

The Take: Presentations should be lively, interesting events that capture and maintain the learners' attention.

The Use: To demonstrate the importance of varying presentation style.

The Patter: "No one would like the reputation this instructor has earned. One of the best ways to avoid this sort of reputation is to vary your presentation style. Aggressively seek ways to capture and maintain the interest of every learner."

Use the space below to record alternative usage ideas.

Alternative Usage Ideas:

Idea 1. _____

Idea 2. _____

Alternative Usage Patter:

Patter 1. _____

_____

Patter 2. _____

_____

Pillow Talk

By Millbower and Yager

I'm ready for your presentation.

Training Topics—Speech/Presentations

The Cartoon: Spell Check

The Captioned Folder Name: SpellCk1

The Captionless Folder Name: SpellCk2

The Subject: Challenges presenter's face.

The Action: A presenter is embarrassed when she misspells a word on the board.

The Take: Misspells happen, especially in an era where computers fix our spelling for us.

The Use: To laugh about possible misspells before they happen.

The Patter: "During your presentation, you may find yourself in this situation. It happens to all of us. Prevent what you can in advance, and don't let mistakes throw you off track."

Use the space below to record alternative usage ideas.

Alternative Usage Ideas:

Idea 1.   _____

Idea 2.   _____

Alternative Usage Patter:

Patter 1. _____

_____

Patter 2. _____

_____

Spell Check

By Millbower and Yager

She should have used spell check.

Training Topics—Speech/Presentations

The Cartoon: Upside Down

The Captioned Folder Name: Upside1

The Captionless Folder Name: Upside2

The Subject: Overhead placement.

The Action: A presenter has placed an overhead upside down on the projector.

The Take: Overheads should be properly set up before the presentation begins.

The Use: As a demonstration of potential presentation problems.

The Patter: "This is one sure way to destroy your credibility before you ever speak. Imagine the difficulty this presenter will have recapturing his audience's attention. Don't let this happen to you. Check your overheads before you begin."

Use the space below to record alternative usage ideas.

Alternative Usage Ideas:

Idea 1. _____

Idea 2. _____

Alternative Usage Patter:

Patter 1. _____

_____

Patter 2. _____

_____

Upside Down

By Millbower and Yager

What does "WELCOME" mean?

Training Topics—Stress Management

The Cartoon: Vacation Relaxation

The Captioned Folder Name: Vacatn1

The Captionless Folder Name: Vacatn2

The Subject: Learning to relax.

The Action: A high profile businessman has gone on vacation, but cannot leave his work behind.

The Take: We sometimes become too wrapped up in our work identity and forget to relax and enjoy ourselves.

The Use: To demonstrate the difficulty people have unwinding from stressful situations.

The Patter: "Some of us are so high strung that we have a difficult time relaxing. As you float on the inner tube of life, remember to leave your suit behind."

Use the space below to record alternative usage ideas.

Alternative Usage Ideas:

Idea 1. _____

Idea 2. _____

Alternative Usage Patter:

Patter 1. _____

_____

Patter 2. _____

_____

Vacation Relaxation

By Millbower and Yager

First day of vacation, huh?

Training Topics—Teamwork

The Cartoon: Bailing

The Captioned Folder Name: Bailing1

The Captionless Folder Name: Bailing2

The Subject: The ramifications of non-teamwork.

The Action: Two people sit in a sinking boat. The person immediately affected by the leak is bailing. The other person is oblivious to the fact that, when the boat sinks, he will also be affected.

The Take: In crisis situations, everyone must work together to solve the problem. Even if it doesn't appear that the problem affects everyone, it often may.

The Use: As a metaphor for the teamwork required for organizational success.

The Patter: "When difficulties arise, it is easy to let the person most directly involved do the work. That may not be the best solution. If a problem is severe enough, it will affect the entire organization. Even if the effect to you is not obvious, sooner or later you may sink too!"

Use the space below to record alternative usage ideas.

Alternative Usage Ideas:

Idea 1. _____

Idea 2. _____

Alternative Usage Patter:

Patter 1. _____

_____

Patter 2. _____

_____

Bailing

By Millbower and Yager

Tell me when it affects my side.

Training Topics—Telecommunications

The Cartoon: While Customers Wait

The Captioned Folder Name: W_Cust1

The Captionless Folder Name: W_Cust2

The Subject: The cause of lengthy customer telephone waits.

The Action: While customers hold, call center personnel engage in personal activities.

The Take: Telephone wait times seem long, and organizations that place callers on hold seem not to care about the callers. This cartoon offers humorous "proof."

The Use: As a reminder of the customer perspective.

The Patter: "Customers rarely understand the cause of lengthy phone waits. In the absence of information, and with idle waiting time on their hands, they imagine all sorts of unrealistic explanations. When you answer calls, remember the customers' frame of mind. Greet them positively, and help them out as quickly as possible."

Use the space below to record alternative usage ideas.

Alternative Usage Ideas:

Idea 1. _____

Idea 2. _____

Alternative Usage Patter:

Patter 1. _____

_____

Patter 2. _____

_____

While Customers Wait

By Millbower and Yager

Please hold for the next available operator . . .

Training Topics—Telecommunications

The Cartoon: Why Rip van Winkle Slept

The Captioned Folder Name: Why_Rip1

The Captionless Folder Name: Why_Rip2

The Subject: Telephone phone trees.

The Action: Rip Van Winkle is sound asleep underneath a tree with a phone at his ear. He fell asleep while waiting on hold.

The Take: It often takes too long for customers to reach a live person.

The Use: As a reminder to customer service representatives that they should move through their calls as quickly as possible.

The Patter: "No one wants to wait on the line. Unfortunately, the volume of calls sometimes means that we can't get to our waiting customers as soon as they would like us to. The best way you can do to help, is to conclude your calls as quickly as possible. We don't want them falling asleep on us."

Use the space below to record alternative usage ideas.

Alternative Usage Ideas:

Idea 1. _____

Idea 2. _____

Alternative Usage Patter:

Patter 1. _____

_____

Patter 2. _____

_____

Why Rip van Winkle Slept

By Millbower and Yager

. . . Please remain on the line for the next available operator . . .

Training Topics—Time Management

The Cartoon: Rock Planner

The Captioned Folder Name: RockPln1

The Captionless Folder Name: RockPln2

The Subject: Successful planning.

The Action: A caveman is chiseling his daily work schedule into a boulder.

The Take: Survival takes planning.

The Use: To reinforce the need for time management.

The Patter: "We tend to view time management as a recent phenomena, but in truth, people have always planned their day. What has changed is the technology that allows us to manage our schedule. Although none of us has to kill a mammoth, planning our time allows us to accomplish the tasks we must complete to survive."

Use the space below to record alternative usage ideas.

Alternative Usage Ideas:

Idea 1. _____

Idea 2. _____

Alternative Usage Patter:

Patter 1. _____

_____

Patter 2. _____

_____

Rock Planner

By Millbower and Yager

Ugh! Busy schedule today.

About the Authors

Lenn Millbower
Through thirty years of extensive study and hands-on experience, Lenn Millbower has discovered practical methods for combining music, entertainment, and learning to create interventions that are creative, meaningful, and fun. He is:

- The author of TRAINING WITH A BEAT: THE TEACHING POWER OF MUSIC, the foremost book on the practical usage of music in learning situations (Stylus Publishing, LLC)
- The composer and musical arranger of DO YOU WANT TO LEARN WITH MUSIC: GAME SHOW THEMES FOR TRAINERS, a CD of original music for trainers (JAM Sessions Music)
- An in-demand speaker, with successful presentations at ASTD International, International Alliance for Learning, International Society for Performance Improvement, and TechKnowledge conferences
- A Learnertainment specialist who as president of Offbeat Training™ is dedicated to helping organizations create learning environments that reach past the noise of daily life
- A dynamic instructional designer and facilitator with years of experience in Entertainment, Walt Disney World, Florida (1985–1999)
- A respected liberal arts educator with experience teaching at all levels
- An accomplished arranger-composer skilled in the psychological application of music to enhance learning
- A popular entertainer with vast performance experience, having traveled throughout the United States, Canada, and the Bahamas as a comedian, magician, and musician

Lenn received his BM in Composition from Berklee College of Music and his MA in Human Resource Development from Webster University. He is a member of the International Alliance for Learning, the National Business Educators Association, the International Society for Performance Improvement, and ASTD.

Doris Yager
Doris Yager is a professional performance coach who has devoted her life to developing the talents of America's youth as they discover the creativity that lives within them. She is:

- The founder, producer, and director of New York's Rhythym-Lite Productions
- An accomplished regional theater show choreographer, including productions of "Guys and Dolls," "Grease," and "Oklahoma"
- A respected show producer, including events at the Lincoln Center and for the City of New York
- A talent scout for the New York City-based T.L.C. Talent agency
- A sought-after dance instructor, having successfully trained three Radio City Rockettes

- A successful show writer and director, with performances at locations as varied as the White House and Walt Disney World
- A developer of talent in all show-business arenas, including performers who have gained success as Broadway performers, radio disc jockeys, musical recording artists, Las Vegas musical directors, and Walt Disney World employees

Doris attended the Munson-Williams-Proctor Institute of Art, the Amarillo Musical Arts Conservatory, and trained for dance with nationally known New York City-based dance instructors. She has been listed among the women civil leaders in the INTERNATIONAL WHO'S WHO OF AMERICA, and is the author of I THOUGHT LIFE WAS A SONG AND DANCE.

Contact Information

Offbeat Training™

Want more information about Offbeat Training™ techniques?

Want to contact Lenn Millbower or Doris Yager?

Visit us on line at

www.offbeattraining.com